The Classical Piano Method

Duet Collection

G000081029

Hans-Günter Heumann

ED 13439

www.schott-music.com

Mainz · London · Madrid · New York · Paris · Prague · Tokyo · Toronto
© 2012 SCHOTT MUSIC GmbH & Co. KG, Mainz · Printed in Germany

ED 13439
British Library Cataloguing-in-Publication-Data.
A catalogue record for this book is available from
the British Library.
ISMN M-2201-3296-4
ISBN 978-1-84761-270-0

Cover design by www.adamhaystudio.com
Cover photography: iStockphoto
Printed in Germany S&Co.8792

CONTENTS

1. Melody No. 3

from *L'ABC du Piano*

Félix Le Couppey (1811-1887)

2. Melody No. 4

from *L'ABC du Piano*

Félix Le Couppey (1811-1887)

Primo

1. Melody No. 3

from *L'ABC du Piano*

Félix Le Couppey (1811-1887)

2. Melody No. 4

from *L'ABC du Piano*

Félix Le Couppey (1811-1887)

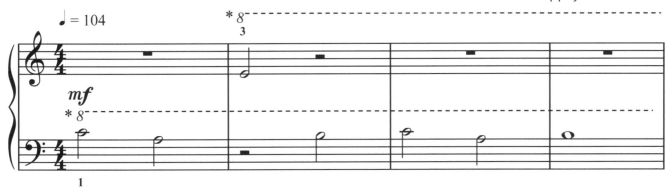

*) With accompaniment, student plays one octave higher than written.

3. In the Light of the Moon

Melody thought to be by
Jean-Baptiste Lully (1632-1687)
Arr.: Hans-Günter Heumann

3. In the Light of the Moon

Melody thought to be by
Jean-Baptiste Lully (1632-1687)
Arr.: Hans-Günter Heumann

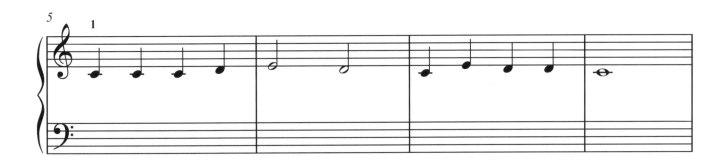

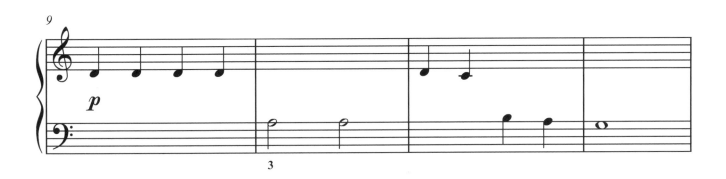

*) With accompaniment, student plays one octave higher than written.

4. Long, Long Ago

Thomas Haynes Bayly (1797-1839)
Arr.: Hans-Günter Heumann

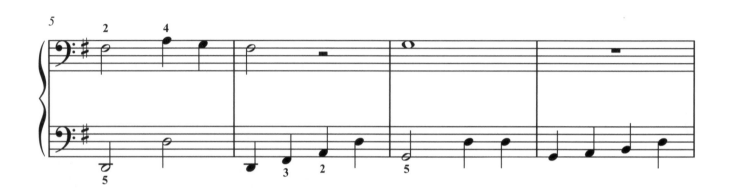

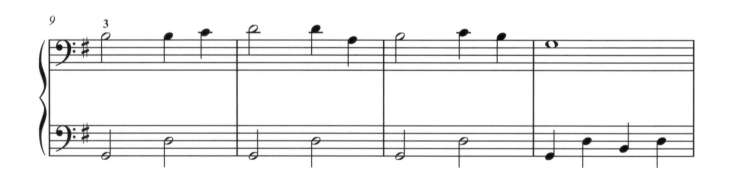

4. Long, Long Ago

Thomas Haynes Bayly (1797-1839)
Arr.: Hans-Günter Heumann

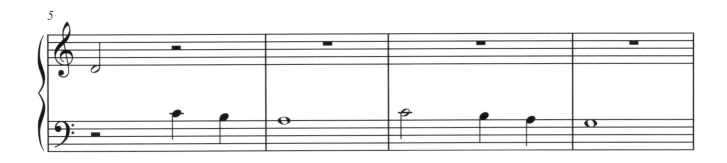

*) With accompaniment, student plays one octave higher than written.

17

21

25

29

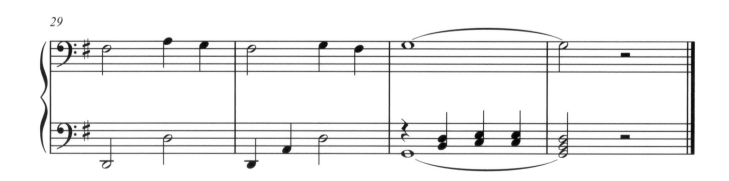

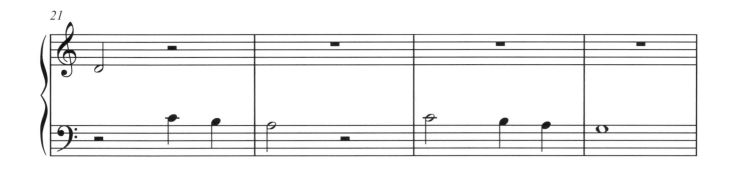

5. Aura Lee

American Folk Song, 1861
Arr.: Hans-Günter Heumann

5. Aura Lee

American Folk Song, 1861
Arr.: Hans-Günter Heumann

6. Big Ben

Bell Tower Melody from England
Arr.: Hans-Günter Heumann

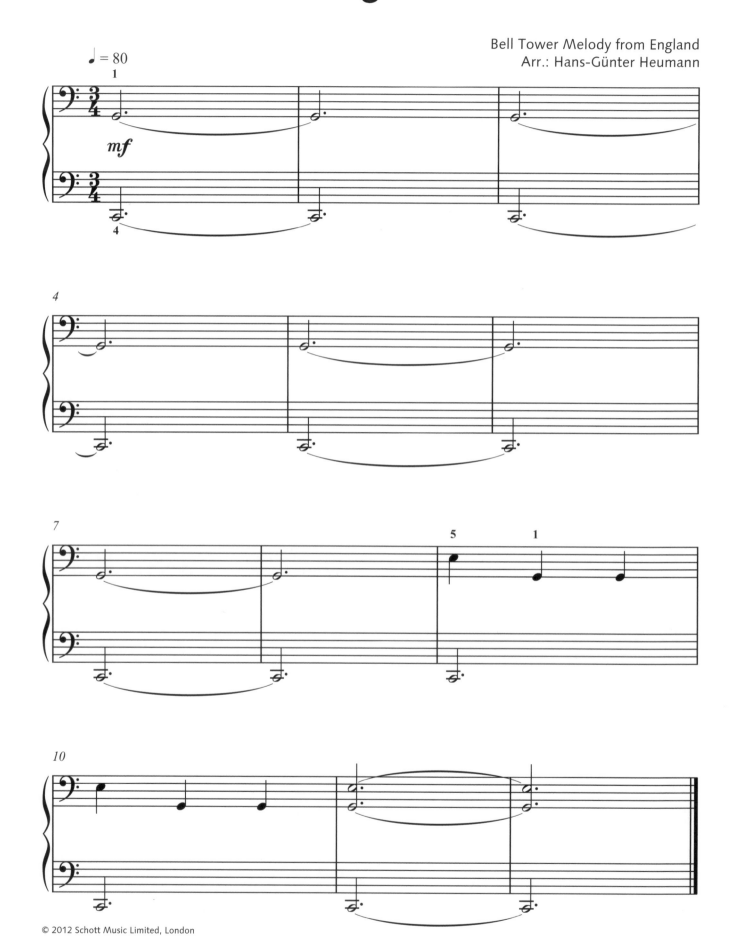

6. Big Ben

Bell Tower Melody from England
Arr.: Hans-Günter Heumann

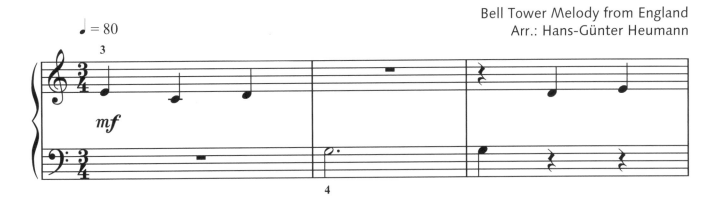

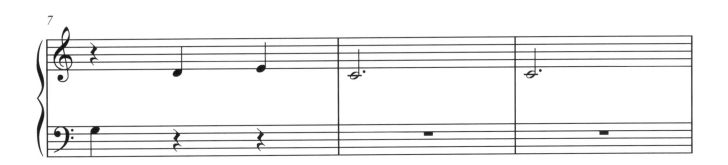

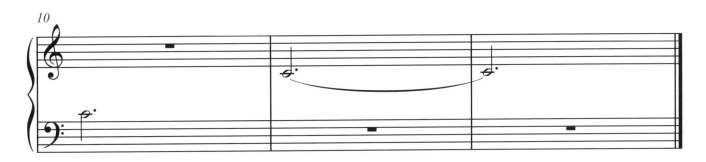

7. O sole mio

Eduardo di Capua (1865-1917)
Arr.: Hans-Günter Heumann

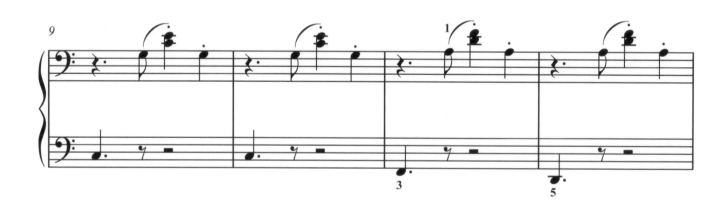

7. O sole mio

Eduardo di Capua (1865-1917)
Arr.: Hans-Günter Heumann

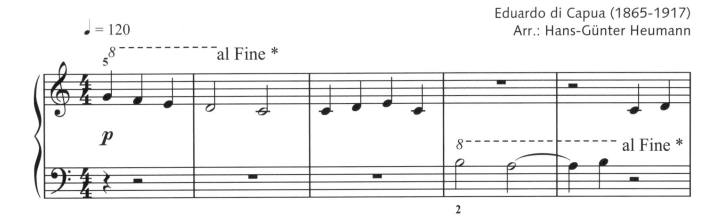

*) With accompaniment, student plays one octave higher than written.

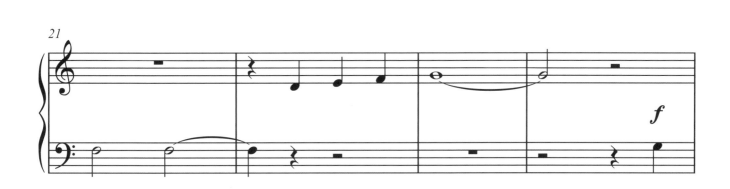

8. Careless Love

Traditional
Arr.: Hans-Günter Heumann

8. Careless Love

Traditional
Arr.: Hans-Günter Heumann

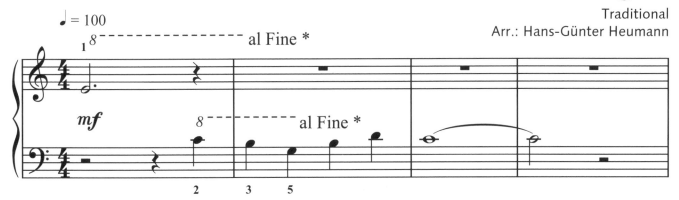

*) With accompaniment, student plays one octave higher than written.

9. The Beginner

Op. 211, No. 1

Cornelius Gurlitt (1820-1901)

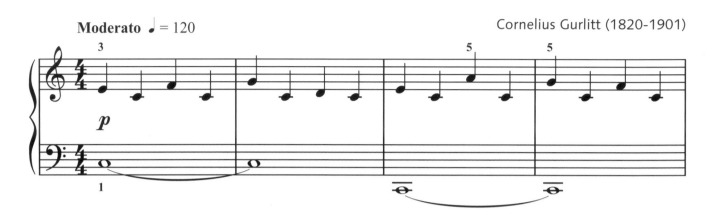

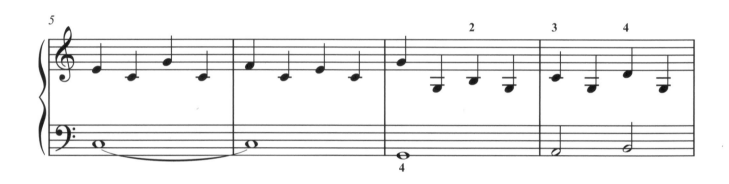

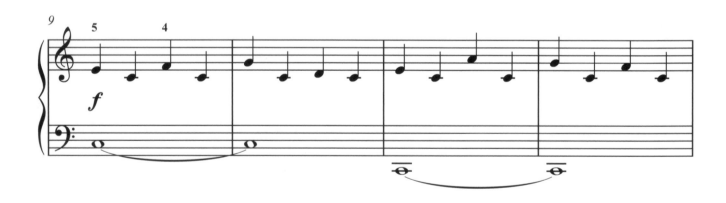

9. The Beginner

Op. 211, No. 1

Moderato ♩ = 120

Cornelius Gurlitt (1820-1901)

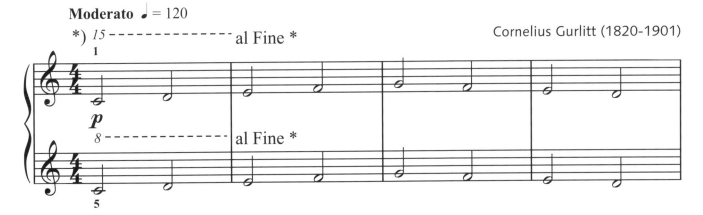

*) When the sign *15⁻⁻⁻⁻⌐* or *15ᵐᵃ* (Ital. quindicesima) appears over a note or group of notes,
play the notes two octaves higher than written.

10. The Musical Children's Friend

Op. 87, No. 1

Heinrich Wohlfahrt (1797-1883)

Non troppo presto ♩ = 184

10. The Musical Children's Friend

Op. 87, No. 1

Heinrich Wohlfahrt (1797-1883)

Non troppo presto ♩ = 184

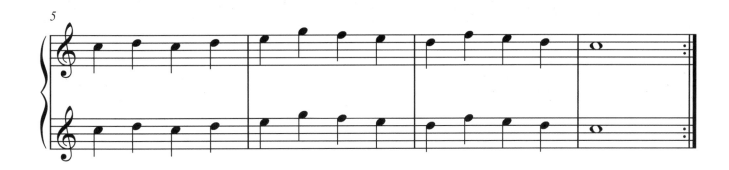

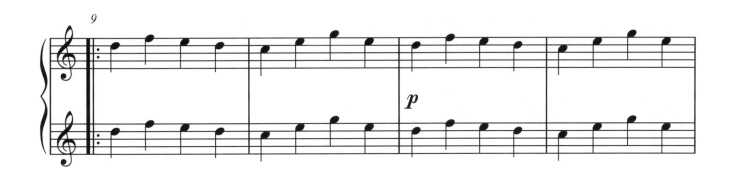

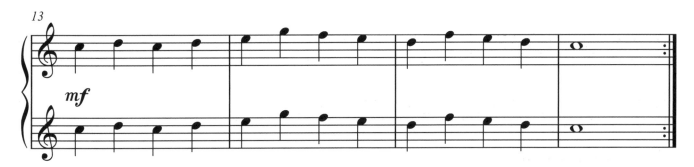

11. Morning Has Broken

Old Gaelic Melody
Arr.: Hans-Günter Heumann

11. Morning Has Broken

Old Gaelic Melody
Arr.: Hans-Günter Heumann

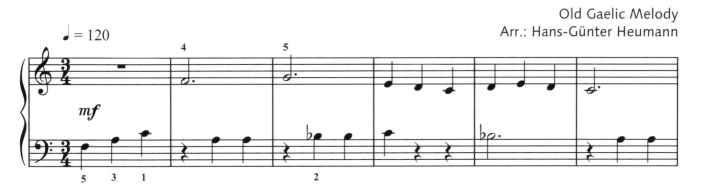

12. Emperor Waltz

Johann Strauss, Jr. (1825-1899)
Arr.: Hans-Günter Heumann

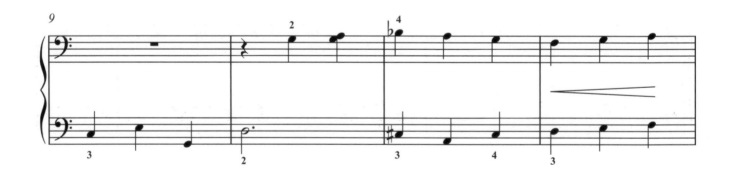

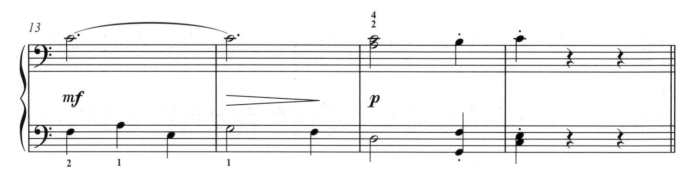

12. Emperor Waltz

♩ = 144

Johann Strauss, Jr. (1825-1899)
Arr.: Hans-Günter Heumann

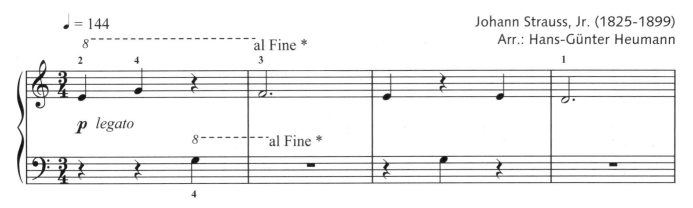

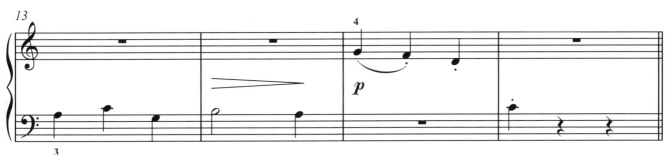

© 2012 Schott Music Limited, London

*) With accompaniment, student plays one octave higher than written.

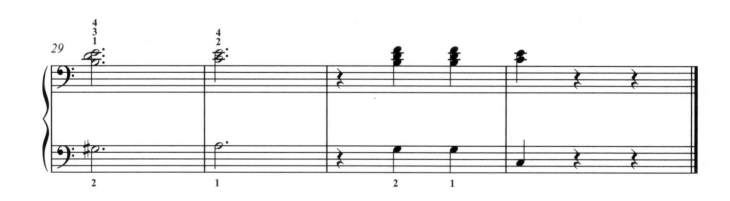

13. Cuckoo, Cuckoo!

♩ = 144

Melody from Austria
Arr.: Hans-Günter Heumann

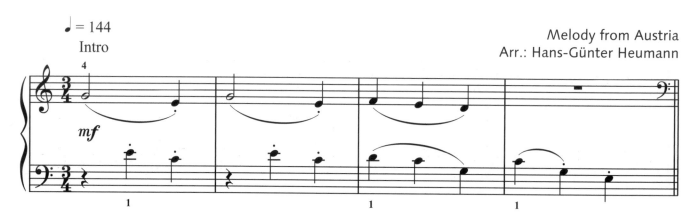

13. Cuckoo, Cuckoo!

Melody from Austria
Arr.: Hans-Günter Heumann

14. Romance

Theme from the 2nd Movement of *A Little Night Music* K 525

Wolfgang Amadeus Mozart (1756-1791)
Arr.: Hans-Günter Heumann

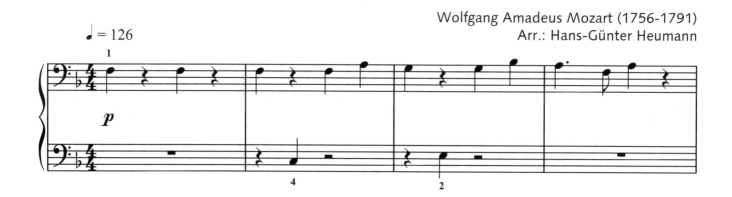

14. Romance

Theme from the 2nd Movement of *A Little Night Music* K 525

Wolfgang Amadeus Mozart (1756-1791)
Arr.: Hans-Günter Heumann

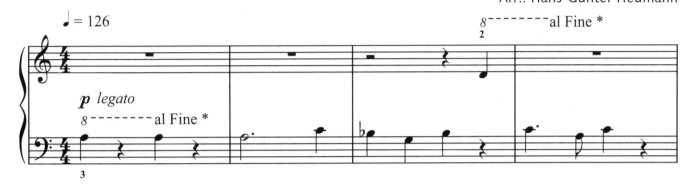

© 2012 Schott Music Limited, London

*) With accompaniment, student plays one octave higher than written.

15. Lullaby

Op. 49, No. 4

Johannes Brahms (1833-1897)
Arr.: Hans-Günter Heumann

15. Lullaby

Op. 49, No. 4

Johannes Brahms (1833-1897)
Arr.: Hans-Günter Heumann

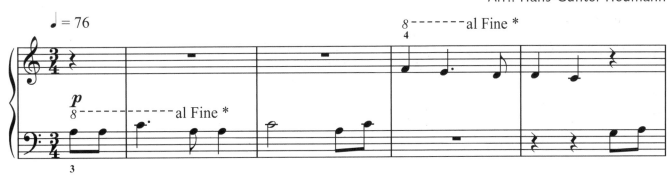

*) With accompaniment, student plays one octave higher than written.

16. Horn Concerto No. 2

Theme from the 3rd Movement K 417

Wolfgang Amadeus Mozart (1756-1791)
Arr.: Hans-Günter Heumann

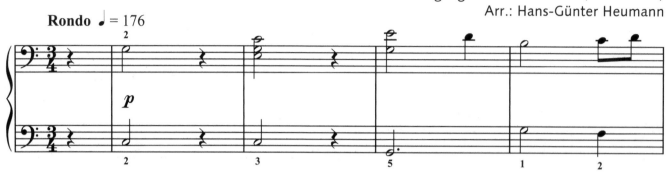

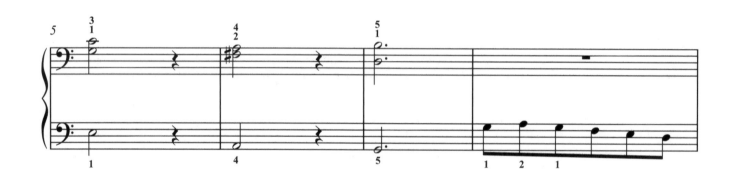

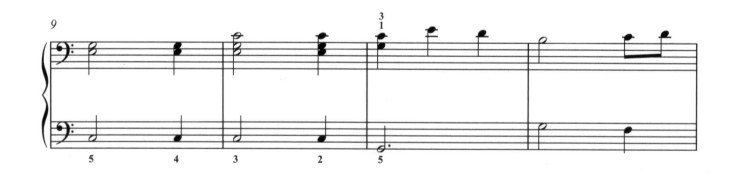

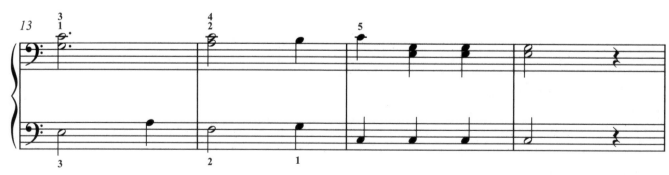

16. Horn Concerto No. 2

Theme from the 3rd Movement K 417

Wolfgang Amadeus Mozart (1756-1791)
Arr.: Hans-Günter Heumann

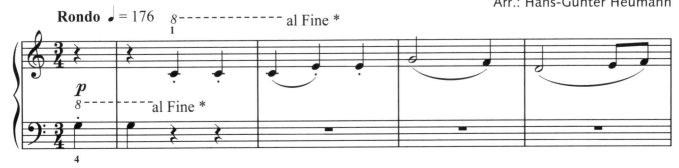

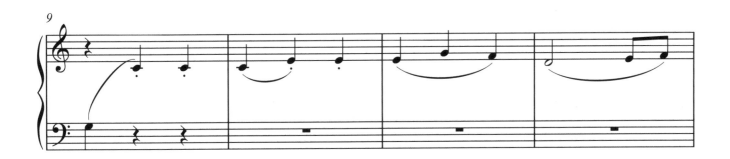

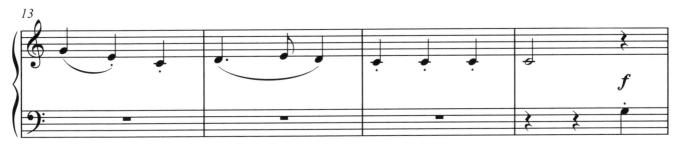

*) With accompaniment, student plays one octave higher than written.

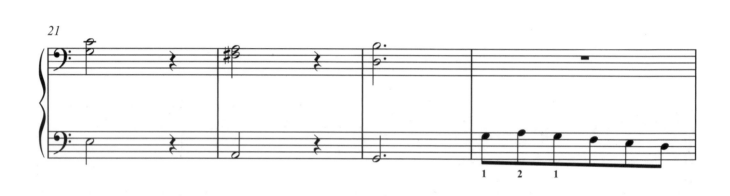

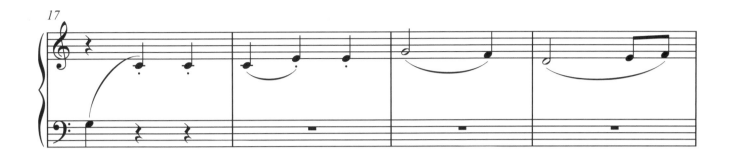

legato

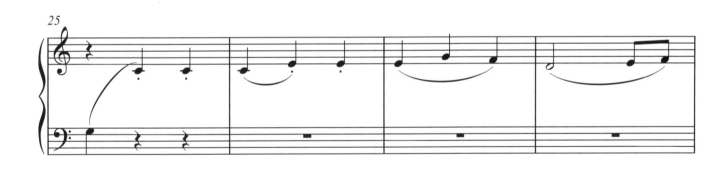

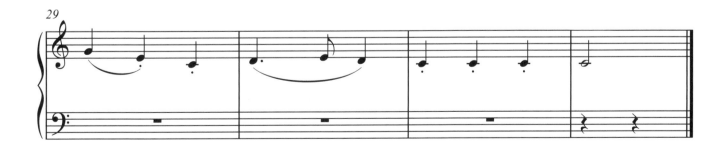

17. Piano Star

Hans-Günter Heumann

17. Piano Star

Hans-Günter Heumann

18. Russian Dance

Trepak

from the Ballet *The Nutcracker*

Pyotr Ilyich Tchaikovsky (1840-1893)

Arr.: Hans-Günter Heumann

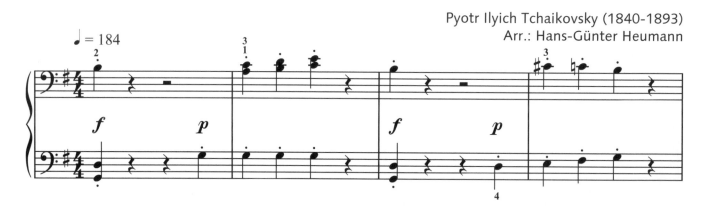

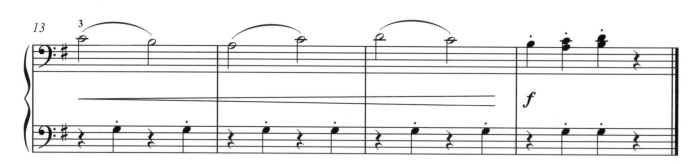

18. Russian Dance

Trepak
from the Ballet *The Nutcracker*

Pyotr Ilyich Tchaikovksy (1840-1893)
Arr.: Hans-Günter Heumann

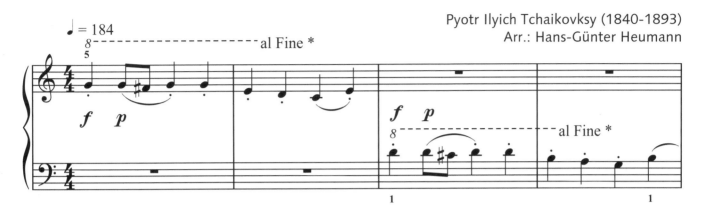

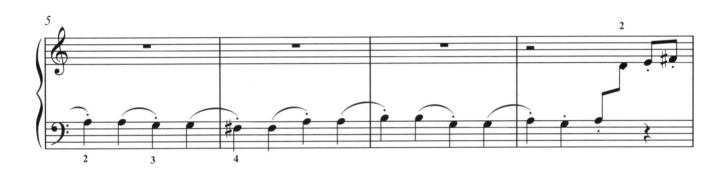

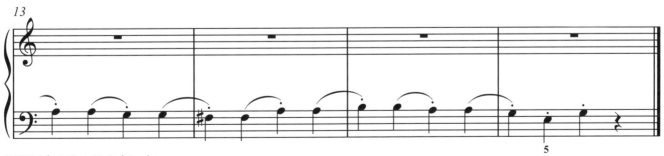

*) With accompaniment, student plays one octave higher than written.

19. The Trout

Op. 32

Franz Schubert (1797-1828)
Arr.: Hans-Günter Heumann

19. The Trout
Op. 32

Franz Schubert (1797-1828)
Arr.: Hans-Günter Heumann

*) With accompaniment, student plays one octave higher than written.

20. The Elephant

from *The Carnival of the Animals*

Camille Saint-Saëns (1835-1921)
Arr.: Hans-Günter Heumann

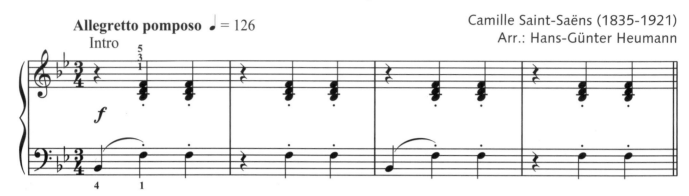

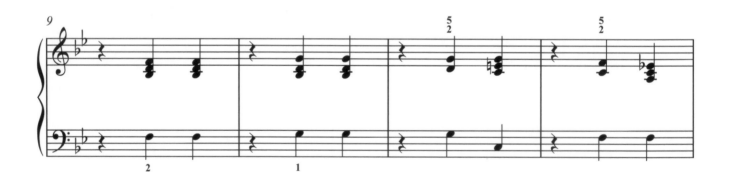

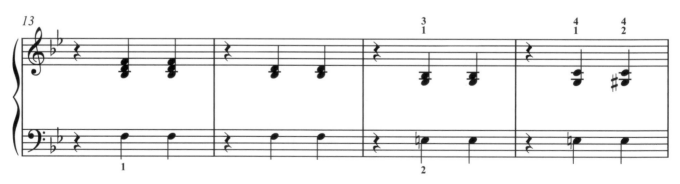

20. The Elephant

from *The Carnival of the Animals*

Allegretto pomposo ♩ = 126

Camille Saint-Saëns (1835-1921)
Arr.: Hans-Günter Heumann

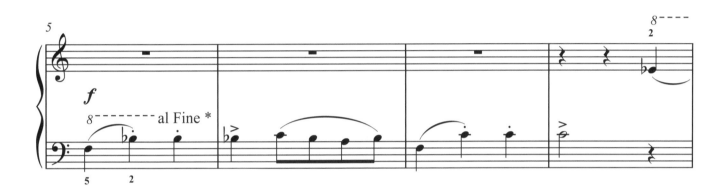

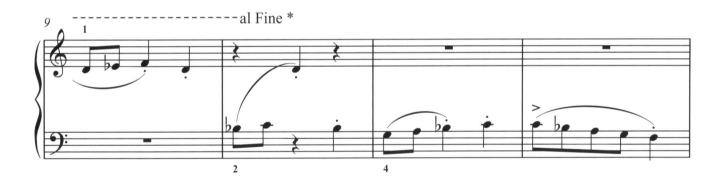

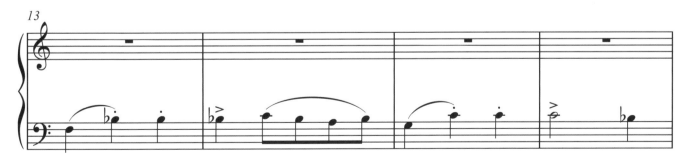

*) With accompaniment, student plays one octave higher than written.

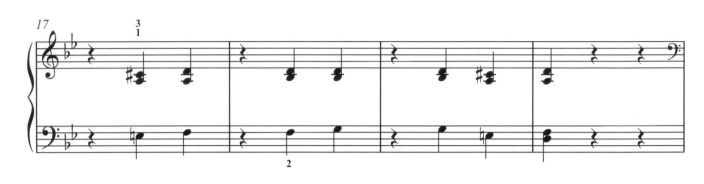

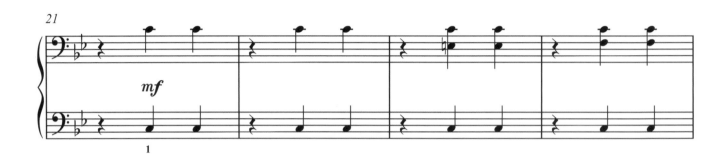

21. The Musical Children's Friend

Op. 87, No. 4

Heinrich Wohlfahrt (1797-1883)

21. The Musical Children's Friend

Op. 87, No. 4

Heinrich Wohlfahrt (1797-1883)

22. The Beginner

Op. 211, No. 3

Cornelius Gurlitt (1820-1901)

22. The Beginner

Op. 211, No. 3

Cornelius Gurlitt (1820-1901)

Allegretto ♩=132

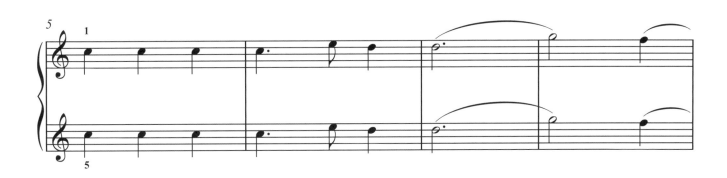

23. Play in the Morning

from *Pieces for Four Hands*

Daniel Gottlob Türk (1750-1813)

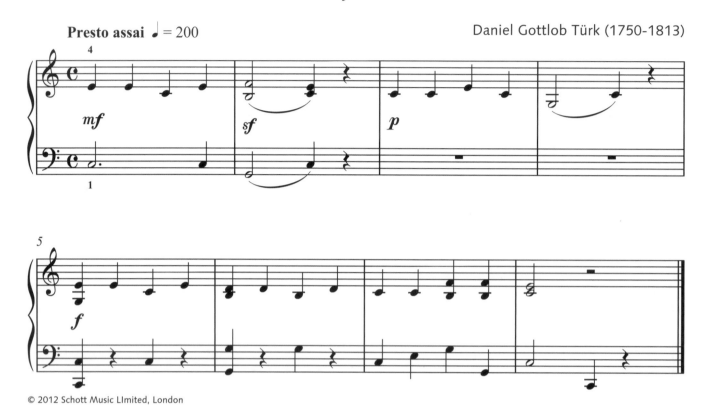

24. Melody No. 5

from *L'ABC du Piano*

Félix Le Couppey (1811-1887)

23. Play in the Morning
from *Pieces for Four Hands*

Daniel Gottlob Türk (1750-1813)

Presto assai ♩ = 200

24. Melody No. 5
from *L'ABC du Piano*

Félix Le Couppey (1811-1887)

♩ = 66

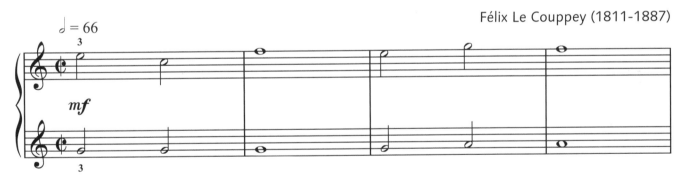

25. Andante

Op. 44, No. 1

Johann Anton André (1775-1842)

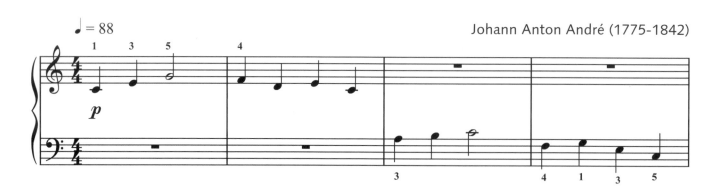

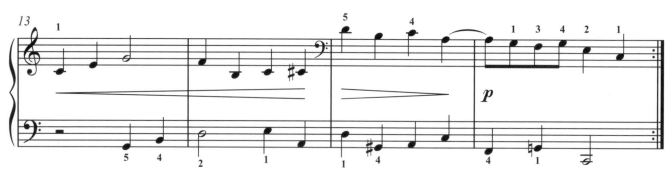

25. Andante

Op. 44, No. 1

Johann Anton André (1775-1842)

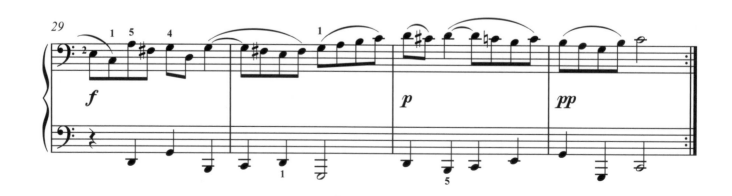

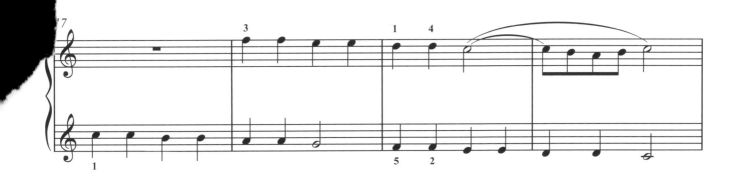

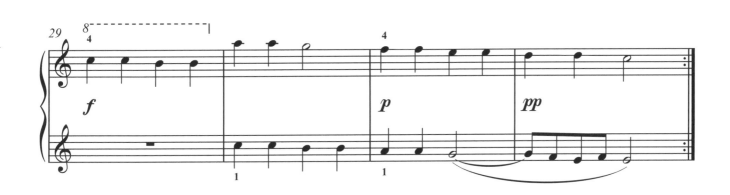

26. The Musical Children's Friend

Op. 87, No. 15

Heinrich Wohlfahrt (1797-1883)

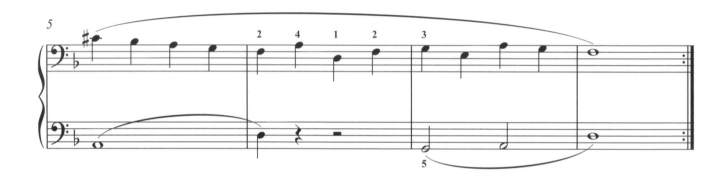

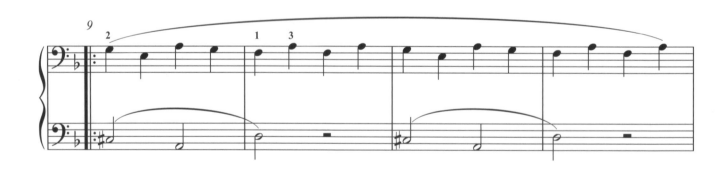

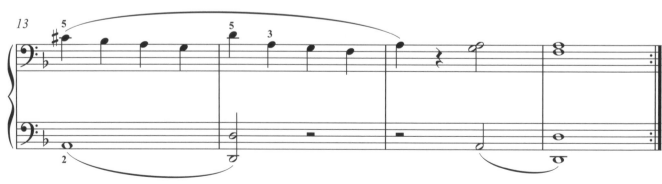

26. The Musical Children's Friend

Op. 87, No. 15

Allegro ♩ = 126

Heinrich Wohlfahrt (1797-1883)

CD Track Listing

1	Melody No. 3
2	Melody No. 3 (Secondo)
3	Melody No. 4
4	Melody No. 4 (Secondo)
5	In the Light of the Moon
6	In the Light of the Moon (Secondo)
7	Long, Long Ago
8	Long, Long Ago (Secondo)
9	Aura Lee
10	Aura Lee (Secondo)
11	Big Ben
12	Big Ben (Secondo)
13	O sole mio
14	O sole mio (Secondo)
15	Careless Love
16	Careless Love (Secondo)
17	The Beginner
18	The Beginner (Secondo)
19	The Musical Children's Friend, No. 1
20	The Musical Children's Friend, No. 1 (Secondo)
21	Morning Has Broken
22	Morning Has Broken (Secondo)
23	Emperor Waltz
24	Emperor Waltz (Secondo)
25	Cuckoo, Cuckoo!
26	Cuckoo, Cuckoo! (Secondo)
27	Romance
28	Romance (Secondo)
29	Lullaby
30	Lullaby (Secondo)
31	Horn Concerto No. 2
32	Horn Concerto No. 2 (Secondo)
33	Piano Star
34	Piano Star (Secondo)
35	Russian Dance
36	Russian Dance (Secondo)
37	The Trout
38	The Trout (Secondo)
39	The Elephant
40	The Elephant (Secondo)
41	The Musical Children's Friend, No. 4
42	The Musical Children's Friend, No. 4 (Secondo)
43	The Beginner
44	The Beginner (Secondo)
45	Play in the Morning
46	Play in the Morning (Secondo)
47	Melody No. 5
48	Melody No. 5 (Secondo)
49	Andante
50	Andante (Secondo)
51	The Musical Children's Friend, No. 15
52	The Musical Children's Friend, No. 15 (Secondo)

Recording Acknowledgments

Recorded October 2011

Piano - Samantha Ward, Maciej Raginia

Engineered and Mixed by Ken Blair, BMP recording

Produced by Ateş Orga